GW00394312

# Introduction

Almost everyone likes walnuts. In fact they're one of Britain's favourite nuts and huge quantities are imported every year, particularly for the Christmas festivities… so why don't we grow our own? Well, the fact is, there's no reason why anyone with space for a tree shouldn't be self-sufficient in these tasty and nutritious nuts.

Walnut trees are really quite easy to grow and require less attention than most conventional fruit trees. This little book will guide you along a clear path to success….so read on!

# NUTSHELL GUIDE to GROWING WALNUTS

Everything you need to know in a nutshell

Clive Simms

Published by
Orchard House Books,
Woodhurst, Essendine,
Stamford, Lincs. PE9 4LQ

**www.orchardhousebooks.com**

**ISBN** 0-9544607-0-7

# How to get started

Before rushing out to buy your walnut tree you need to know a few facts that will help you decide on the right one for you.

- The botanical name for the walnut common in the UK is *Juglans regia.* This is only one species from many found around the world, eg. *Juglans nigra* is the black walnut of North America.
- Walnut trees grow between 10m to18m tall and may live 200 years or more.

- *Juglans regia* is not native to the British Isles but originated in Persia. Although introduced here centuries ago it's still prone to our frosty spring weather killing the tender early shoots.
- Damp, rainy climates such as ours encourage leaf diseases.
- Some walnut trees don't crop well if grown alone as a single tree.
- Walnut trees grown from seed are often poor producers of walnuts and are best avoided.

Fortunately, over the years many walnut trees have been selected, named and propagated. Some are ideal for our climate and overcome most of the difficulties mentioned above. Such trees also begin to produce nuts quickly, often within two or three years. They will cost more than seedling trees but are so superior that you should consider purchasing nothing less.

# Rootstocks

When you buy a named walnut it will be a grafted tree where a small piece of the parent tree or cultivar will have been united onto the roots of another young walnut tree. The only rootstock used at the moment for this purpose is seedling *Juglans regia*. This always produces full sized trees. Unlike most fruit trees no true dwarfing rootstock is yet available for walnuts. *Juglans nigra* rootstock has been used in the past for its dwarfing effect, but it can give rise to a fatal virus problem called 'black line' so it's not a good idea. If space is limited it's best to choose a less vigorous cultivar.

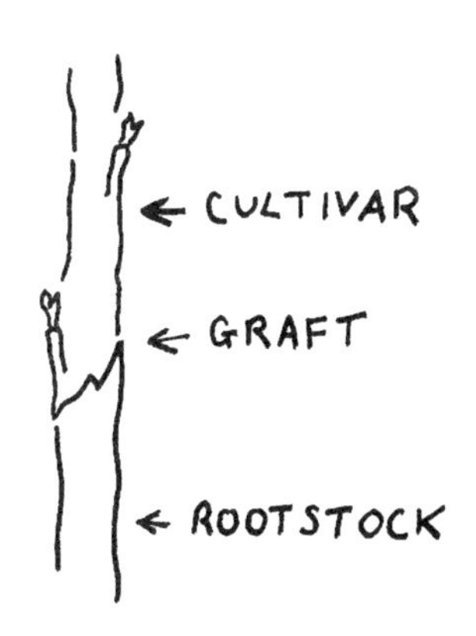

# Pollination



Theoretically, all walnuts are self-fertile; that is, they fruit when grown by themselves. Male catkins and female flowers both appear at the tips of the new growth in spring. However, matters are complicated because some trees produce their male and female flowers at slightly different times. Biologically, this ensures cross-pollination takes place with another tree, but from a nut grower's point of view it's a nuisance, as it requires two trees to be planted to ensure a nut crop.

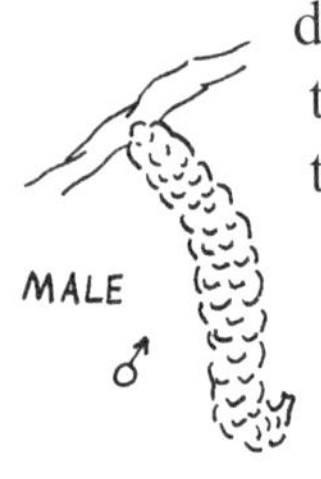


Happily, self-fertile trees that bear both male and female flowers at the same time are available. Other trees are partially self-fertile, with the two bloom times overlapping sufficiently to allow a reasonable crop to be produced without the need for a nearby pollinator. Obviously, partially self-fertile trees tend to have heavier crops if pollen from an unrelated tree is available.

The male catkins produce lots of bright yellow pollen that's distributed by the wind.

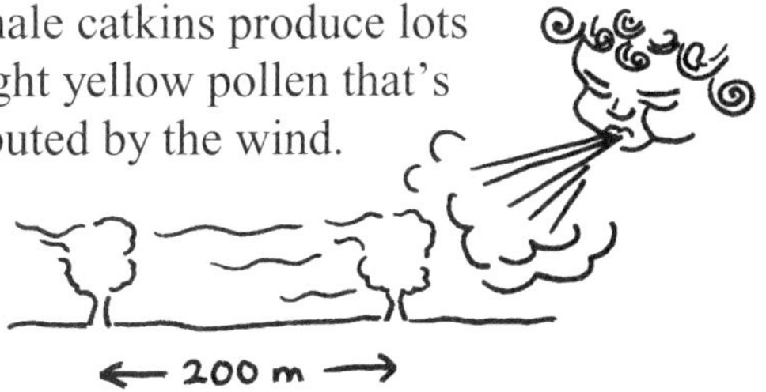

← 200 m →

Trees up to 200m away may act as pollinators for your tree (if required) providing the wind is blowing in the right direction.

A few walnut trees exhibit an uncommon process called apomixis. This enables the female flowers to develop into nuts without pollination. The cultivars 'Number 26' and 'Number 139' (see page 14) in particular display this useful trait and this probably accounts for their regular cropping habit.

# Site

Walnut trees do well in loamy, slightly alkaline soils. They require a regular supply of water, especially during the growing season, but a poorly drained, waterlogged site is to be avoided.

They're best suited to the milder southern parts of the country where a site well protected from cold winds and late spring frosts is ideal. Northern locations and low-lying frost-hollows do present difficulties, but don't despair! If you obtain one of the very late leafing cultivars available that are likely to miss late spring frosts you should be OK (see pages 13 & 14).

Squirrels are a nuisance to nut growers! If they're common in your area they need to be taken into account when siting your tree (see page 26 & 27 for details).

Bear in mind that walnut husks rot down to give a slippery black mess that can cause staining if brought into the house on shoes. It's best to plant your tree away from paths and utility areas.

# Buying your tree

Trees may be bought from garden centres and nurseries at any time of year if growing in a pot or container, whilst bare-rooted trees are only available after being dug up in the winter when dormant. They should be clearly labelled with the cultivar name, eg. **Walnut (*Juglans regia*) 'Broadview'**. If such information is lacking be on your guard….they're likely to be merely seedling trees.

If your local garden centre or nursery can't provide what you want then you may have to obtain a tree by mail order from a specialist supplier. It will normally be sent to you in a bare-rooted condition sometime between November and March. If it arrives when you're unable to plant it simply dig a small hole somewhere in the garden and cover the roots with soil to keep them moist until you have time to deal with it properly. Make sure that rabbits or deer can't nibble your new tree!

The names of possible suppliers of good walnut trees may be found in the current edition of 'The Plant Finder' which is available at most booksellers. Those with access to the Internet can do this by visiting www.rhs.org.uk

## Which to choose?

The following are the walnut cultivars most suitable for British gardeners. All have good quality nuts but vary in their time of leafing out, disease resistance and mature height. Most are self-fertile.

**Broadview:** A relatively compact tree. Late-leafing. Disease-resistant foliage. Partially self-fertile.
**Buccaneer:** Vigorous, upright tree. Late-leafing. Disease-resistant foliage. Self-fertile.

**Hansen:** A smaller tree. Leafs out a little early so some risk from frost. Disease-resistant foliage.
**Number 26:** Vigorous upright tree. Very late-leafing, little risk from frost. Disease-resistant foliage. Self-fertile. Tends to show apomixis (see page 9).
**Number 139:** Moderately late-leafing. Self-fertile. Strong tendency for apomixis.
**Rita:** A smaller tree. Early-leafing so at risk from frost. Self-fertile.
**Soleze:** Late-leafing. Partially self-fertile.

# Planting

A small tree, around 1m to 1.5m in height is best. This size of tree tends to establish itself much more quickly than a larger specimen and is less prone to being blown over by the wind before the roots have grown sufficiently to hold it firmly in the ground.

Autumn is the ideal time of year for planting as the ground hasn't yet completely cooled down and some root growth will occur before the onset of winter. Alternatively, it's fine to plant anytime over the winter period (weather allowing!) but before the tree starts to show signs of growth in spring. Always be generous with the size of planting hole to allow the roots to spread out. A little extra work now pays dividends in the future. It isn't necessary to add fertiliser when planting, although a kilogram of bone meal added while back filling provides plenty of phosphorus to stimulate root growth. Make sure you firm the earth down with your feet to ensure the roots are in close contact with the soil.

Staking may not be required if your tree is small and on a sheltered site, but a 1m temporary stake for the first couple of years is usually found to be helpful. Drive the stake in first before planting to avoid spearing the young roots. Never underestimate the power of the wind and always use a stake that's up to the job. This may be of wood or metal but check that when the tree is tied to it no rubbing takes place. The tie should be made of something soft which gives a little, old tights are ideal! Don't use wire or twine; you'll probably forget to slacken it as growth takes place and the constriction will cause damage.

In the spring following planting a handful or two of general purpose inorganic fertiliser, or a little well-rotted manure or compost, should be spread around the tree but clear of the trunk.

Grass and weeds compete for minerals and water, so keep a circle of about 1.25m diameter around the tree clear of vegetation for the first few years. This may be done by spraying with herbicide or placing mulching mats of plastic or old carpet around the base of the trunk.

Drought is the commonest reason for young trees dying. Walnuts respond well to generous watering during the growing season so keep your hosepipe handy!

If the planting site is well fenced and netted against rabbits and hares you may get away without using a rabbit guard, although they cost so little it's cheap insurance and gives peace of mind.



If deer are around you must take measures to protect against their browsing. Deer fencing the site will solve the problem, but it is expensive. The usual solution is to place a tree tube around each tree, which will also give protection against rabbits.

The 1.2m tube most commonly available is slightly too short to completely prevent deer nipping out the growing tip. Taller 1.5m tubes are available, or you can simply telescope two together to give the extra height. If you do this make sure they are fixed firmly or the top one may slip down exposing the tree.

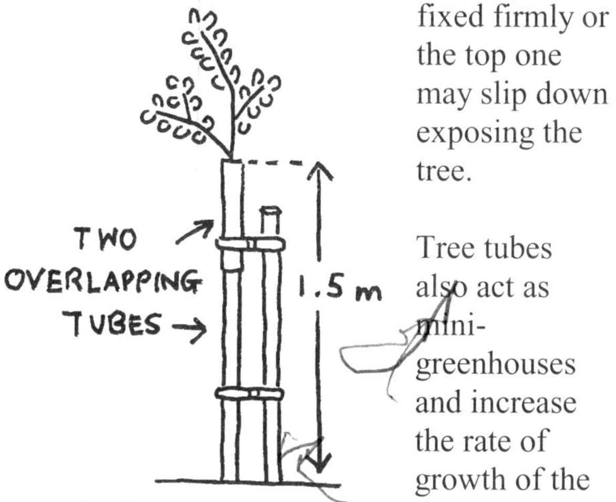


Tree tubes also act as mini-greenhouses and increase the rate of growth of the tree. Unfortunately, they can also be death traps for small birds that fall in and are unable to escape. It's best to cover the top with mesh until such time as the tree grows out.

If more than one tree is planted allow at least 9m between them. Up to 15m isn't excessive, particularly if the trees are known to be vigorous growing types.

# Feeding

As the tree grows it benefits from an annual feed of compost or inorganic fertiliser. A spring feed of 0.5kg of 10-10-10 NPK or similar fertiliser for each 3cm of the trunk's diameter will keep it growing strongly. This is available from any garden centre. The feed should be applied evenly over the area of ground covered by the spread of the branches and is best done when rain is imminent.

A generous application of compost or animal manure is an excellent way of supplying the required minerals… with the additional benefit of also feeding the soil and helping maintain a rich population of useful micro-organisms. Leaf mould, although low in nutrients, is a first class soil conditioner and encourages a myriad of beneficial soil organisms in a completely natural way.

# Pruning

Walnut trees are usually grown so as to have a trunk of about 2m to 2.5m before branching occurs. Initial pruning aims to create a straight and clean trunk with four or five widely spread branches radiating out to form the crown. Subsequent pruning only requires the removal of any dead or crossing branches and any that spoil the symmetry of the tree.

Pruning should be carried out in winter while the tree is dormant. Any major pruning undertaken while the tree is in growth will result in copious amounts of sap 'bleeding' from the wound. This is unlikely to kill the tree but is distressing to see!

## Pests & diseases

Walnuts are relatively disease free, the only problems being leaf blotch and walnut blight. **Leaf blotch**, also called anthracnose, is a fungal disease caused by a species of *Mycosphaerella* (also known as *Gnomonia leptostyla* or *Marssonina juglandis*) and shows itself as small brown-black spots on the leaves and young nuts that then enlarge to become dirty yellow blotches. In severe cases the leaves and nuts fall off prematurely. It occurs most readily in wet spring weather and is common in Britain. It's not usually a major problem and may be controlled with fungicidal sprays and raking up and disposing of affected leaf litter in the autumn. Planting resistant cultivars is always worth considering in our damp climate.

**Walnut blight** (*Xanthomonas juglandis*) is a potentially serious bacterial disease but fairly uncommon in Britain. It causes die-back of small branches and loss of crop. Symptoms are small black angular spots on the leaves and fruit. Attacks are worse if cool wet weather occurs during flowering. Late flowering cultivars are most likely to escape attack. Spraying with Bordeaux mixture at fortnightly intervals between bud break and the end of July gives some control.

Small areas of blister-like swellings on the leaves frequently cause concern. These are galls caused by infestations of a microscopic ***Eriophyid*** mite. Fortunately, the damage is mainly cosmetic and best ignored.

The worst pests facing the British nut-grower are undoubtedly **rooks** and **grey squirrels**. **Rooks** become interested in walnuts as the husks split open to reveal the ripe nut. They may be detected by the presence of small pieces of broken walnut shell appearing on the ground under the branches, or more obviously by a squawking flock of rooks circling around the tree. Little can be done about this apart from scaring the birds away by whatever means you have at your disposal. Rooks are intelligent birds and very wary of man so a frequently moved scarecrow may help, as will intermittent loud noises, although these could also scare the neighbours!

Using a long pole to shake the tree and get the harvest in quickly is always a sound strategy. The amount of nuts lost due to rooks depends much on your situation, but obviously planting a walnut tree near to a rookery is not a good idea.

The **grey squirrel**, not to be confused with the increasingly rare and protected native red squirrel, is a common garden pest that shows a great interest in walnuts when the nuts are beginning to ripen around mid-September.

Although a cute and entertaining animal the grey squirrel is no friend of the nut-grower, and if a crop is to be had some measures must be taken to outwit them. Poison baits and trapping, the usual tactics employed by commercial foresters and nut growers, are inappropriate and distasteful for amateurs.

Your best strategy is to concentrate on denying access to the ripening crop by initially positioning your tree well away from buildings or other trees that allow convenient jumping off points for squirrels. The recommended distance to prevent this happening is 3m, but obviously the more space the better. The advantage of training your walnut tree to have a straight trunk of about 2m to 2.5m lies not only in it allowing easy passage underneath for grass-cutting, but in giving sufficient space to fix a **squirrel baffle** to the trunk at harvest time. As soon as clear signs of raiding are seen, such as mounting piles of gnawed nutshell beneath the tree or favourite perch, you need to put your baffles in place.

## Here's how to do it

Attach overlapping pieces of thin sheet metal around the trunk of the tree to form a continuous band. The sheets need to be around 1m tall and placed at least 1.5m up

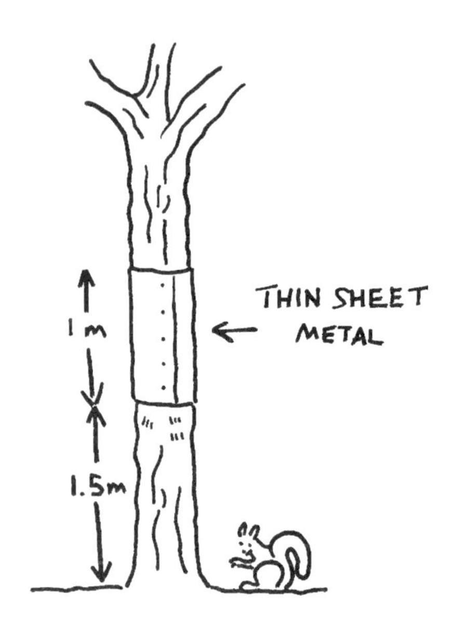


from ground level. This prevents the squirrel jumping over the baffle from the ground and is tall enough to form a barrier as it climbs the tree trunk. If sheets are overlapped make sure that the upper sheet goes over the lower to prevent a toehold being formed. The metal sheets are too smooth for the squirrel to grip.

Used aluminium lithographic plates, obtainable from commercial printers, are excellent for this job and may be temporarily fixed onto the tree with small nails and removed once the harvest period is over.

Even with a baffle in place squirrels will still forage underneath your tree looking for fallen nuts. A simple ruse to counter this is to place containers of soil near to the tree for the squirrel to use to bury the booty. You then dig them up and reclaim what's yours!

# Harvesting

Walnut trees may provide two crops each year as the unripe nuts are pickled in mid-summer well before the ripe nuts are gathered in autumn. If pickled walnuts are to your taste they're well worth doing, being easily made but relatively expensive to buy.

Nuts for pickling should be gathered around late June or early July before the developing shell becomes hard. Test them with a skewer; if you can't push it through the nut you've left it too late!

Ripe walnuts will begin to fall from the tree in autumn, usually late September or early October. When ripe, the green husk splits open releasing the nut to fall to the ground.

Irritatingly, there are always some nuts where the husk, or part of the husk, remains firmly attached. If the husk isn't removed it will decay and stain the entire nut and contents black. Therefore, collect them as soon as they fall and clean and rinse them using a soft brush. It's a good idea to shake the tree at this time and collect the bulk of the crop quickly, so avoiding animal pests enjoying the harvest too. Always wear rubber gloves when handling wet walnuts as the juice from the husks stains human skin an unattractive nicotine brown that's hard to remove!

Walnuts should be dried quickly to prevent them going mouldy. Do this by circulating warm air (approx. 20°C) over them for a couple of days, or put them on top of a warm stove. Care is required at this stage; if the nuts overheat they'll spoil, and if dried for too long they become hard and brittle.

# Last words

That's it!

Now all you have to do is put this knowledge into practice and in a few years you too could have an attractive shady tree to relax under on hot summer days, your own walnuts to share with friends at Christmas, and the satisfaction of growing a magnificent green legacy for the future.

## Good luck!